MISS WITHERSPOON

BY CHRISTOPHER DURANG

★

DRAMATISTS
PLAY SERVICE
INC.

MISS WITHERSPOON was commissioned by McCarter Theatre (Emily Mann, Artistic Director; Jeffrey Woodward, Managing Director; Mara Isaacs, Producing Director) in Princeton, New Jersey, in 2004, and was then co-produced by McCarter and by Playwrights Horizons (Tim Sanford, Artistic Director; Leslie Marcus, Managing Director; William Russo, General Manager). It premiered at McCarter on September 9, 2005, and the same production and cast opened at Playwrights Horizons on November 11, 2005. It was directed by Emily Mann; the set design was by David Korins; the costume design was by Jess Goldstein; the lighting design was by Jeff Croiter; the sound design was by Darren L. West; the production stage manager was Alison Cote; and the assistant stage manager was Christine Whalen. The cast was as follows:

VERONICA .... Kristine Nielsen
MARYAMMA .... Mahira Kakkar
MOTHER 1 AND MOTHER 2 .... Colleen Werthmann
FATHER 1, FATHER 2, SLEAZY MAN,
DOG OWNER, WISE MAN .... Jeremy Shamos
TEACHER, WOMAN IN A HAT .... Linda Gravatt

CHARACTERS

VERONICA — smart but worried woman, mid-forties to late fifties. Her nickname, we learn, is Miss Witherspoon.

MARYAMMA — a spirit guide in the netherworld. She may be any age, but she is intelligent, and has grace of movement and loveliness of spirit. She is also forceful when she needs to be. She wears a sari, and her ethnicity is Indian (that is, from India).

MOTHER 1 — thirties, a new mother somewhere in Connecticut. Thrilled to have her new baby, sensible, nice.

FATHER 1 — thirties, married to Mother 1. Also thrilled to have their first baby. He looks prosperous in a good suit, and probably works in the financial district. Sensible, nice.

MOTHER 2 — thirties, drug addict much of the time; cranky to have a baby. Might dress in tank top and cut-offs. Not trying to be mean, but not fighting it either.

FATHER 2 — Hell's Angel type, married to Mother 2. Drooping moustache, long hair, jean jacket, boots. Also a drug addict. Less consistently mean than Mother 2, but it's partially because he zones out a lot.

TEACHER — any age, but best forty to fifty-five. African-American. A bit overworked, but a good teacher, intelligent, wants to help when she can. Though she knows she needs to set limits or she'll go crazy.

DOG OWNER — nice guy, thirties. Pretty average, has a girlfriend but they don't live together. Loves his dog.

SOOTHING VOICE — a soothing voice.

WOMAN IN A HAT — African-American. A surprise visitor in the netherworld. Proud of her appearance, wears an impressive "going-to-church" hat. Sassy and pointed in her comments.

WISE MAN — another visitor in the netherworld. Long white robes, he is an articulate and somewhat powerful wizard.

In production, the following roles are doubled:

MOTHER 1 and MOTHER 2 are played by the same actress.

TEACHER and WOMAN IN A HAT are played by the same actress.

FATHER 1, FATHER 2, SLEAZY MAN, DOG OWNER, SOOTHING VOICE, and WISE MAN are played by the same actor.

TIME

Recent past, foreseeable future.
(1998, 2005 and beyond)

PLACE

Earth, and not earth.

MISS WITHERSPOON

Scene 1

Lights up on Veronica. She is seated in a chair by a small telephone table. She is on the phone. She is in her late forties, maybe early fifties. Pleasant, in a nice skirt and blouse. Maybe once she worked in publishing. She has an undercurrent of sadness some of the time.

VERONICA. *(Into phone.)* Well, that's just me. Kind of overwhelmed, kinda blue. That's how I am, I'm too old to change. Oh, just things. No, I don't see him anymore. That's long gone. I'm really done with him. I'm kind of done with everything, actually. *(Listens, repeats back.)* Look to the future. *(She laughs.)* Oh, I'm sorry, I thought you were making a joke. Oh, you weren't. *(Tries a bit to entertain this comment.)* Look to the future. You mean, other men? Hope? I find it hard to get on the hope bandwagon, I always have. *(Listens.)* I've tried the antidepressants. They don't work. I'm antidepressant-resistant. *(Listens; irritated now.)*

Well, no I haven't tried *every single one.* Listen, dear, I know I called you, and you're a dear person, but I think I shouldn't have called. I think I'm not in the mood to talk. I just need to go to the grocery store or something. Don't be offended, alright? *(Listens.)*

Well, if you're going to be offended, then it just proves I can't get on with anybody, and that's kind of depressing to me. *(Listens, very irritated.)* Please stop talking about Zoloft! I've got to hang up. Please just understand who I am. I can't change. *I don't want to change.* Bye, dear, talk to you … sometime. *(Hangs up; laughs. Frowns. Suddenly feels very sad, lost in thought. Throws off her thoughts, picks up pad and pencil that are on the telephone table.)*

(Lights up on a larger area, which represents the outside, perhaps a

small garden she keeps. Veronica leaves the chair area, and walks out-side. The light is softer, there are the sounds of a few birds, it's restful. Veronica listens, and her whole body relaxes. She starts to write on the pad. Writing the following down:)

Eggs, butter, cheese. Bread, milk, frozen vegetables. Peas, carrots. String beans. (Suddenly a large "thing" drops from the sky, falling near where Veronica is. It seems to be metal and very heavy, and it makes a big clank when it falls. Or sound creates the large clank. Screams:)

AAAAAAAAAAAAAAAAGGGGHHHHH! (Veronica stares at the object, alarmed and startled. Looks up to the sky. Moves a bit forward, tentatively. Doesn't know what to do. Goes back to her list.)

Paper towels, tuna fish, mayonnaise. (A smaller object falls. Less scary, but nonetheless something falling. Veronica lets out a smaller yelp.) ... Aaaaaaa! Goodness. (Looks up again.)

(A woman in a chicken suit comes running out.)

WOMAN IN CHICKEN SUIT. The sky is falling! The sky is falling!
VERONICA. What?
WOMAN IN CHICKEN SUIT. The sky is falling! It's falling! (Runs off in terror.)
VERONICA. What do you mean? (She looks worried, concerned. A third big "thing" falls down on the other side of her. This one is quite big and thus quite scary.)

AAAAAAAAAAAAAAAAAAAAGGGGGHHHH! (She goes over to the object, looks at it. Looks upward again to see if there are more coming. She feels very afraid. She looks more closely at this third fallen object. Then she looks upward again.)

Stop falling! (Suddenly a fourth object falls from the sky with a big thud. And then a fifth object almost immediately afterward. Both terrorize her, but the fifth one frightens her even more — she wasn't expecting the fifth one so close after the fourth one. She throws her pad and pencil into the air, and runs off screaming. Running off screaming:)

AAAAAAAAAAAAAAAAAGHHHHH!

(Lights dim to black. The sound of falling objects continues, intensifies. Scary, loud, disorienting. Silence for a bit. The crashing of heavy objects from the sky seems to have stopped. Quiet. There is the sound of waves for a bit, soft, but that dies down too.)

Scene 2

Lights come back on. Veronica is found standing in a pool of light. She speaks to the audience.

Well, I'm dead. I committed suicide in the 1990s because of Skylab. Well, not entirely, but it's as sensible an explanation as anything.

~~Most of you don't remember what Skylab was ... I seem to have had a disproportionate reaction to it, most people seemed to have sluffed it off.~~

Skylab was this American space station, it was thousands of tons of heavy metal, and it got put up into orbit over the earth sometime in the 70s.

~~Eventually the people onboard abandoned it, and it was just floating up there; and~~ you'd think the people who put it up there would have had a plan for how to get it back to earth again, but they didn't. Or the plan failed, or something; and in 1979 they announced that Skylab would eventually be falling from the sky in a little bit — this massive thing the size of a city block might come crashing down on your head as you stood in line at Bloomingdale's or sat by your suburban pool, or as you were crossing the George Washington Bridge, etc. etc.

Of course, STATISTICALLY the likelihood of Skylab hitting you on the head — or rather hitting a whole bunch of you on the head — statistically the odds were small.

But I can't live my life by statistics.

And the experts didn't think it through, I guess. Sure, let's put massive tonnage up in the sky, I'm sure it won't fall down. Sure, let's build nuclear power plants, I'm sure we'll figure out what to do with radioactive waste *eventually.*

Well, you can start to see I have the kind of personality that might kill myself.

I mean, throw in unhappy relationships and a kind of dark, depressive tinge to my psychology, and something like Skylab just sends me over the edge.

"I CAN'T LIVE IN A WORLD WHERE THERE IS

SKYLAB!" — ~~I sort of screamed this out~~ in the airport as I was in ~~some endless line waiting to go away to somewhere or other.~~

So I died sometime in the 90s. Obviously it was a *delayed* reaction to Skylab.

~~So I killed myself. Anger turned inward, they say. But at least I got to miss 9/11.~~

~~If I couldn't stand Skylab, I definitely couldn't stand the sight of people jumping out of windows. And then letters with anthrax postmarked from Trenton. And in some quarters people danced in the streets in celebration. "Oh, lots of people killed, yippee, yippee, yippee." God, I hate human beings. I'm glad I killed myself.~~

~~You know, in the afterlife I'm considered to have a bad attitude.~~

And apparently I'm slated to be reincarnated and come do this horrible thing again.

Why can't I just be left alone to fester and brood in my bodiless spirit state? Who says spirits have to be clear and light and happy? So what if my aura looks like some murky brown tweed suit? So what? ~~Leave me alone, and I'll leave you alone.~~

~~Anyway, they tried to *force* me back onto earth in 2002 or so, and before I knew it my spirit was starting to reincarnate, but I put on some sort of spiritual otherworldly emergency brake system that I seem to have, and the whole process came to a grinding halt, and I simply REFUSED to reincarnate.~~

"What if I marry Rex Harrison again?" I said to them. ~~Or maybe next time he'll be my mother and I'll get so frustrated maybe I'll go off the deep end and commit matricide. Or then there will be more Skylabs. And of course terrorism and anthrax and smallpox and monkey pox and a pox on everybody's houses. So, no thank you.~~

Yes, I was married to Rex Harrison. He had several wives, so you'll have to do research to figure out which one I was.

I really don't want to come back. I just find too much of it all too upsetting.

~~So~~ I'm refusing to reincarnate, ~~at least as much as I can. I didn't like being alive, I don't trust it.~~ Plus, you know, if I can keep thwarting these attempts to reincarnate me, I'm not sure the earth is going to still be there, so if I stall long enough, my going back may become a moot point. *(Looks at the audience, realizes what she said.)* I'm sorry, am I depressing everyone? ~~I'm depressing myself.~~

Well, pay no attention, I'm just a gloomy dead person, there's no ~~accounting for my moods, I guess I was bipolar in life, and I still am out here in the afterlife.~~

~~Is there anything positive to leave you with?~~ (*Tries to think of something positive, has trouble thinking of anything; then tries this as a positive wish:*) ~~Well, good luck. I mean it sincerely. I guess life has always been scary — Hitler was scary, I was a child then; and we all expected to die from Russia and America aiming missiles at one another, and that didn't happen. So good luck — maybe it'll be all right. I hope it will. I just don't want to come back, but if I hear it all has worked out a bit better than we expected, well, I'll be glad. So long.~~ (*Lights dim on her. Maybe sounds of water. Then a light wind.*)

Scene 3

Lights up. Veronica is seated on a chair, but is asleep, having a mild nightmare. She is in the bardo, a kind of netherworld. Like images of heaven, this netherworld is filled with a beautiful blue — blue sky or blue non-realistic background. The chair she sits in is in the shape of a traditional chair, but it might be see-through. You can see its shape, but sometimes she seems to be sitting on air. Some quirks may be added to this netherworld. Pretty lanterns might be lowered from the sky [Attached to what? Who knows?]. Also if there are any other furniture or design elements, they should seem Eastern — from India, Thailand, etc. In her sleep, having a bad dream:

VERONICA. Look out, look out! Help! Help!

(*Enter an Indian woman — from India, that is, not Native American. Her name is Maryamma. She is dressed in a beautiful sari of rich, deep colors. She is attractive and smart, but also has a sharp edge to her.*)

MARYAMMA. Come on now. Miss Witherspoon, wake up. Come on, wake up.
VERONICA. What? What? (*Wakes.*) Oh, it's you again. Leave me alone, please.

MARYAMMA. You have a lot more lessons to learn, you're still focusing on your past life, or arguing with your ex-husband, you have a lot more lives to do, Miss Witherspoon.

VERONICA. My name isn't Miss Witherspoon.

MARYAMMA. Well, we like to call you Miss Witherspoon. It's our nickname for your spirit. You're like some negative English woman in an Agatha Christie book who everybody finds bothersome. It's because of your brown tweed aura. You have a lot of aura cleansing to do in future lives, you know.

VERONICA. Aura cleansing. I don't know what that means.

MARYAMMA. My aura is light and airy and clear, Miss Witherspoon. Maybe after a few more lifetimes you'll be able to accurately see other people's auras.

VERONICA. I've explained as patiently as I can that I don't wish to go back to earth. Can't I just be left alone?

MARYAMMA. That's not how the netherworld works, Miss Witherspoon.

VERONICA. Is there someone above you I can speak to?

MARYAMMA. We don't think of people being above or below each other here. We're all part of the collective human soul.

VERONICA. Okay. But might I speak to some *other* member of the collective human soul, I don't feel you're understanding me.

MARYAMMA. Who do you want to speak to?

VERONICA. I don't know. Is Mahatma Gandhi here?

MARYAMMA. Yes, he is. But your soul is in no way ready to meet him.

VERONICA. What's your name, I want to report you.

MARYAMMA. To whom would you report me?

VERONICA. Well, I don't know that now, but maybe later on it will become clear. What is your name?

MARYAMMA. I've told you before, I'm Maryamma.

VERONICA. Maryanna what?

MARYAMMA. I don't have a last name. And it's Mar*yamma*, not Mary*anna* … The middle letters are not "n" as in Nancy, but "m" as in mellifluous … Mary — *yamma*.

VERONICA. You know, I'm a Christian. I wasn't expecting some sort of Eastern religion person to greet me up here. I mean, I know a lot of American companies are hiring people in India to do phone work for them, but I wasn't expecting to find that in the afterlife as well.

MARYAMMA. There is no ethnicity in the bardo. That is just how you are choosing to see my spirit.

VERONICA. Really? Well, I've imagined you in a very pretty sari.

MARYAMMA. Yes, and I appreciate it. But you know for the last thirty years of your life, you had no religion. And so your spirit is choosing to see me as an Indian woman because your soul is acknowledging reincarnation.

VERONICA. If there has to be an afterlife, I demand the pearly gates, and St. Peter. And purgatory if I have to. And heaven so I can rest there. And I don't believe in hell.

MARYAMMA. Well, that's very convenient for you. But even the people who see St. Peter, reincarnate. Purgatory is actually reincarnation, that's why it lasts so long and has suffering in it. It's going back to earth and struggling over and over.

VERONICA. I don't believe you. You find some priest or minister to tell me that.

MARYAMMA. And sometimes St. Peter looks like the traditional idea of him, robe and beard and all of that. And sometimes he looks like a Hawaiian man. And sometimes, in the last many years, he looks like E.T. or Yoda. The effect of movies on the collective unconscious —

VERONICA. I don't trust anything you're saying.

MARYAMMA. But you've had many lives already. You haven't just had one.

VERONICA. I don't believe you.

MARYAMMA. Yes. Remember 1692 in Massachusetts? Your sister was put to death as a witch. You knew it wasn't true, but you didn't speak up for her.

VERONICA. Well, of course. I would have been killed.

MARYAMMA. Oh, so you remember?

VERONICA. No, I don't remember. I was speaking from common sense. *If* I had been there, that's what I would've thought. I've seen *The Crucible*, it was a terrible time. Doesn't mean I lived then.

MARYAMMA. Well, you did. And you were a dance hall hostess in Wyoming in 1853. And you were a cloistered nun in 1497 in Düsseldorf.

VERONICA. Düsseldorf? I don't believe you. And I certainly remember nothing.

MARYAMMA. You're just stubborn. Think back. You can remember all the other lives up here in the bardo, when you want to. It's back on earth you can't remember them, or just remember little pieces of them. Remember the song "Where or When?"

VERONICA. Yes, it was very pretty, but it was about a small

13

hotel, it wasn't about reincarnation.

MARYAMMA. You're confusing it with "There's a Small Hotel." "Where or When" was indeed about reincarnation. *(Sings.)*
> *It seems we've stood and talked like this before,*
> *We looked at each other in the same way then*
> *But I can't remember where or when …*

VERONICA. That's about forgetful lovers, it's not about reincarnation.

MARYAMMA. It IS about reincarnation.

VERONICA. I know Mary Rodgers, the daughter of Richard Rodgers, and I'm going to ask her to write you a letter explaining "Where or When" to you.

MARYAMMA. There's no way a letter can be delivered in the bardo.

VERONICA. You keep saying the bardo, but you don't say what you mean. What is the bardo?

MARYAMMA. It's where you are now. It's a stopping-off place where you can choose your next life, and then drink from the Lake of Forgetfulness before you return to the earth plane again.

VERONICA. Drink from the Lake of Forgetfulness. You're some terrible dream I'm having. If this is the afterlife, I demand to see St. Peter. And not the E.T. one either.

MARYAMMA. You don't really qualify as a Christian, in your last life you stopped believing in it early on, so demanding to go to Christian heaven is not your right after this past lifetime.

VERONICA. Ah, so there *is* a Christian heaven?

MARYAMMA. Yes. For those who believe in it, there is. And there's a pet heaven. And a Muslim heaven. And a Jewish heaven which, since they don't believe in an afterlife, is kind of like prolonged general anesthesia.

VERONICA. Oh, I want that one! Send me to that one.

MARYAMMA. Your soul automatically chooses the image of heaven it wishes to see. You may be telling me you want to see St. Peter, but your soul has chosen that you see me and I need to get you to reincarnate. And none of those funny shenanigans about stopping it from happening this time.

VERONICA. It's scary down there, and it's painful, and if you want me to learn some lesson or other, well, give me a book and I'll read it. *But I don't want to go back there.*

MARYAMMA. It's not your choice. All souls must keep reincarnating until they reach true wisdom at which point they sometimes go back to guide others — like Gandhi did — or sometimes they reach nirvana, and their spirit permeates and uplifts the collective unconscious.

VERONICA. Just leave me at this level, I'm not harming anybody, just let me rest here in the ... bardo.

MARYAMMA. I've told you that cannot be your choice.

VERONICA. Well, I've stopped it several times so far, haven't I?

MARYAMMA. That's true. We're all a little confused by that. The force of your will has been creating a little glitch up here, and the reincarnation process keeps aborting itself with you. We've asked Gandalf to look into that so that your next reincarnation actually occurs.

VERONICA. Gandalf? Isn't he a fictional figure from *The Lord of the Rings?*

MARYAMMA. Yes, there is the fictional character Gandalf. But he in turn was based on a real person of great wisdom also named Gandalf, who's lived many centuries, and who's very involved with helping souls to continue their evolution in the bardo and back on earth.

VERONICA. I wonder if I'm in a coma and I'm dreaming you.

MARYAMMA. Life is the dream.

VERONICA. Yes, yes, I've heard that before. It's very confusing. I don't wish to play these games. I want that Jewish heaven which is like general anesthesia. I want to be put out like a light.

MARYAMMA. You only get that when your soul believes in no afterlife. But even then it's an illusion ... you are in that blank state for a while, but after a bit, your soul still reincarnates, and eventually most souls on earth begin to believe in some sort of afterlife. After all, as Thornton Wilder said, everybody knows in their bones that *something* is eternal.

VERONICA. I like Thornton Wilder. Is he here?

MARYAMMA. Yes, but he's presently reincarnated.

VERONICA. Really? As who?

MARYAMMA. As Arianna Huffington.

VERONICA. I don't believe Thornton Wilder is Arianna Huffington.

MARYAMMA. No, I was kidding. Thornton Wilder has achieved nirvana, and is no longer reincarnating, but his soul sends out wonderful vibrations throughout the entire universe.

VERONICA. There's an Indian restaurant on West Fifty-ninth Street that overlooks Central Park South, and it's called Nirvana.

MARYAMMA. And your point is?

VERONICA. No point, I guess. I'm feeling tired, my brain hurts.

Can I be allowed to sleep a little more?

MARYAMMA. Yes, your spirit depletes quickly, you need to achieve more stamina.

VERONICA. Easier said than done, Maryamma nirvana-head. Oh, gosh, my eyes are so heavy. *(She falls asleep. Maryamma exits quietly, wanting her to sleep.)*

(Lights dim and perhaps change color. We hear the sound of wind whooshing. A spotlight comes up on Veronica. It's bright and the rest of the stage is dim or a vastly different color. It's like there's a wind machine underneath her ... her clothes are being blown strongly, and hair. There might be a light from underneath her too ... it's like she's flying through space and time back to earth. She stays seated in her chair, holding on for dear life, as her body and especially legs are being drawn to the side, into some vortex that is the entry back to a life on earth. Note: Most of this should be done by the actress herself, with body movements. During the whooshing:)

Oh God, it's happening again. No, thank you. I don't want to go. I'm not going. *(She makes facial grimaces, resisting being pulled down to earth.)* Stop it now. Hell no, I won't go! Hey, hey, LBJ, how many kids did you kill today? God, what am I talking about? Stop it! I won't go back! Stop it! *(The spotlight goes out on Veronica. The whooshing sound stops. There is the sound of a baby crying. It's pretty dim on stage.)*

Scene 4

Then lights up. A nursery. Veronica is in a bassinet with a baby bonnet on her head. She looks ahead with a baby's innocent, uncertain look. Her face looks its correct age, of course, but she is now a curious, normally happy baby.

Looking fondly at the baby in the bassinet is the mother. She is dressed tastefully and is clearly middle-to upper-middle class. Mother is probably thirties, pleasant, happy to have a baby.

Note: This is an "on earth" setting, but it should not take up the whole stage space, especially if you have a normal-sized theatre. It should either be a small set of a bedroom that lives within the larger bardo set, or it could perhaps be done with just a few pieces of furniture and lighting. For this scene the bassinet is especially important.

MOTHER. Hello, darling. Hello there. Yes. It's Mommy. Hello. Good morning. How did precious sleep?
VERONICA. Ga ga. Goo goo. Ma-ma-ma! Ma-ma-ma!
MOTHER. Yes, Mama!

[Note: the actress playing Veronica should not attempt to do "realistic baby sounds." She should do the "ga ga, goo goo" sounds as if that is how babies indeed speak at that age. A bit like having an actor playing a dog say "woof, woof," rather than imitating a real bark. And the "baby lines" should indeed sound a bit babyish, and should be said quickly.]

VERONICA. Ma-ma-ma! Ma-ma-ma!
MOTHER. One less syllable, dear. Ma-ma.
VERONICA. Ma-ma-ma! Ma-ma-ma! *(To herself, her adult voice.)* Oh God, I'm a baby again. Oh Lord, no, I can't go through this again, it's endless.
MOTHER. What, dear?
VERONICA. *(Baby talk sounds.)* Google, google.

17

MOTHER. Yes, Google, that's a search engine. Oh, David, she's very chatty this morning. She almost said Mama.

(Enter David, the father. Thirties. He's in a suit, dressed for work. Also pleasant, a bit prosperous. Also happy to have a baby.)

FATHER. Talkative, is she? Good morning, sweet pea.
VERONICA. Goo goo, la la la la.
FATHER. That's right, darling, very good. What a beautiful baby. *(Sound of dog barking, then growling.)*
MOTHER. Oh David, don't let Fido in here.
VERONICA. *(Her adult voice, to herself.)* "Fido" — give me a break. *(Calls out upward, adult voice still.)* Someone get me out of here!
MOTHER. Oh, she seems restless. Are you restless, darling?
VERONICA. *(Assenting to question.)* Ga ga ga! Ma-ma.
MOTHER. Oh she said Ma-ma. Yes, darling. I'm Ma-ma. *(Sound of dog growling. The actors playing Mother and Father can play that the dog has entered the room, pretend he's present.)* David, take Fido out. I think he's jealous of the baby.
FATHER. He's just not used to her yet. He'll learn to accept her.
MOTHER. Well, he doesn't usually show his teeth, I don't like that.
VERONICA. *(With a glint; baby voice, but awfully articulate.)* Doggie! Like doggie! Let him stay! *(Mother and Father are speechless.)*
MOTHER. Good God, did you hear that? She formed real sentences.
FATHER. Did we imagine it?
MOTHER. I don't think so. Darling, did you say doggie? Doggie?
VERONICA. *(Trying to get them off track.)* Googie. Ga ga.
MOTHER. Maybe she said googie and it sounded like doggie.
FATHER. That must have been it. Is that what you said, little Miss Witherspoon? *(Veronica looks startled.)*
MOTHER. David, what did you call her?
FATHER. I'm not certain. It was just an impulse. You know that nursery rhyme, whither the spoon goes, whither the fork.
MOTHER. Whither the spoon? I've never heard that nursery rhyme.
FATHER. No, neither have I, come to think of it. *(Dog growls again.)* Fido, no! *(Slaps dog's nose, seemingly.)*
MOTHER. Well, don't hit the dog, David. Just leave him outside.
FATHER. Alright. Out in the hallway, Fido. Go find your ball. Go on. *(Dog apparently leaves; Father turns back to Mother.)* So you don't want to call her Miss Witherspoon?
MOTHER. What? Are you insane?

FATHER. Well, you choose the name, I'm clearly out of my league. Goodbye, sweet pea, see you tonight. Daddy's off to business.

MOTHER. Oh, darling, I'll see you to the car. There are some things I want you to pick up on your way home. *(Mother and Father leave. Veronica looks bored.)*

VERONICA. Ga ga ga. Moooooo. La la la. *(Adult voice.)* Oh God, I have to relearn language. It takes so long. Why am I remembering everything? *(Dog growls. Dog has apparently come back in the room. Veronica looks very interested.)* Oh. Oh, yes. *(Combination of baby and adult voice; gets glint of purpose.)* Ga ga, here, doggie. Here, doggie. Come here, Fido. I'm taking your place in the house. Come here. Here, doggie. *(More growling.)* Oh yes, big teeth. Very big teeth. Here, doggie, come here, come here. *(Veronica makes her neck available to the dog. Barking sounds continue. Blackout. Terrible dog barking sounds in the dark. Wind whooshing, ocean breaking on the waves — and then boom!)*

Scene 5

Lights back on, Veronica arrives back in the bardo.

VERONICA. I'm back, I'm back, hooray, hooray! *(Maryamma comes rushing in, angry.)*

MARYAMMA. What did you just do?

VERONICA. I'm back!

MARYAMMA. Did you just commit suicide at two weeks old?

VERONICA. It wasn't my fault. You sent me where there was a vicious dog.

MARYAMMA. Yes, but you chose ... Oh forget it, that was a wasted lifetime. And that poor couple are going to suffer and have guilt, and try to make it up with the next child who's going to be spoiled and will take no responsibility for anything and then will get drunk at age sixteen and drive a car without a license and kill two people — you see what you've done?

VERONICA. I didn't do it. If that's how they behave, that's how they behave, it's not my fault.

MARYAMMA. Your aura is worse than before.

VERONICA. Look, I was thinking. I don't want St. Peter. I want to go to the Jewish heaven which is like general anesthesia. Can you arrange that, please?

MARYAMMA. This isn't a spa.

VERONICA. Not only do I not like life on earth, I realize I don't like to be conscious. I don't want to be here talking to you. I would consider it a wonderful favor if you could arrange for me to be put under.

MARYAMMA. The general anesthesia afterlife is just what happens to the people who don't believe in an afterlife. And you can't just choose the Jewish heaven. Plus I sort of misspoke. It's not only Jewish people. It's also people like Jean-Paul Sartre and Camus. You know, people who don't believe in an afterlife.

VERONICA. I want blankness, I want nothing.

MARYAMMA. Between grief and nothing, I'd choose grief, William Faulkner wrote. Later Jean-Paul Belmondo took the same quote in the movie *Breathless* and said, "I'd choose nothing."

VERONICA. *(Brief pause.)* Why are you telling me this?

MARYAMMA. What you said just made me think of it, that's all. You're choosing nothing. It's a negative choice, nothing. People who go to a restaurant and order nothing, don't eat. Their bodies don't get nourishment. Nothing is as nothing does.

VERONICA. I don't remember those lines in *Breathless.*

MARYAMMA. Oh, you saw the film?

VERONICA. I didn't see the Godard version. I saw the Richard Gere remake on HBO one night.

MARYAMMA. I hate when they make remakes of classic films. It's terrible. It's like when someone says a beautiful sentence, and then some jerk later on comes and says, let me paraphrase that for you.

VERONICA. Yes, Rex always hated remakes too. Gosh, even saying his name makes me angry. Is there a hell and can you check if he's there?

MARYAMMA. What do you have against Rex Harrison?

VERONICA. I told you, I was married to him. And he wasn't very nice.

MARYAMMA. I explained before, you were married to the soul of Rex Harrison but not when he was Rex Harrison. He had similarities, but he was a coal miner in 1876. In your last life you kept recognizing him when you'd see the actor Rex Harrison, but you were actually recognizing your husband from 1876 not the person who won the Oscar for *My Fair Lady.*

20

VERONICA. What are you talking about? I remember *going* to the Oscars with Rex Harrison.

MARYAMMA. You're blurring memories, dreams and fantasies. It's partially that brown tweed aura of yours, thoughts get stuck in it.

VERONICA. I thought you said we could remember our past lives up here.

MARYAMMA. I did. But people are all on different levels of development, and because of your continuing negative choices, your level of development is fairly messed up.

VERONICA. You're very critical, and you're not very encouraging. I'd like you to go away now, and if I can't be under general anesthesia, then I'd just like to sit and stare and try to think nothing for a while. *(Veronica sits in her chair, hoping to end the conversation and to zone out for a while.)*

MARYAMMA. Well, two years have gone by since we started this conversation …

VERONICA. What?

MARYAMMA. So it's time for you to reincarnate again.

VERONICA. It can't be. I just got here.

MARYAMMA. Goodbye. *(Maryamma exits. Whooshing sounds again. Veronica is suddenly in that same place [her chair] — the air whooshing up at her hair, the light from below, sounds of rushing through air, being sucked downward. Once again her legs are being pulled by some force, back down to earth. Lights dim or almost go to black on Veronica.)*

Scene 6

Lights come up on a second mother and father. They are played by the same actors who played the previous mother and father, but they look and seem very different. Mother 2 and Father 2 are of a lower social class. Indeed they are trailer trash. Mother 2 has a cigarette dangling, and coughs a lot. Father 2 is a Hell's Angel type. Long hair, dirty T-shirt. Leather jacket probably.

[Note: Let's avoid making them sound Southern. Think instead of angry "super-size" people in Ohio, or upstate New York. Maybe Monticello, New York. And they can also be angry thin people, too. Just not Southern.]

If there's a setting, it should look run-down and depressing. Veronica once again is a baby, and is in a new bassinet, and is wearing a dirty baby's cap. The bassinet may not be a regular bassinet. It may be a tin washing tub, or something like that.

MOTHER 2. Hey, baby. Gee, it's kind of a fat baby, isn't it?

FATHER 2. Yeah, it's gonna have your fat ass.

MOTHER 2. Shut up. It's gonna have your greasy hair and damaged brain cells.

FATHER 2. Yeah, well, I had fun damaging them.

MOTHER 2. Good for you. Why isn't the baby responding? Is it dead? Are you dead? *(Yells.)* HEY, BABY! Hey, fat-ass! You dead? *(Veronica has been looking around, kind of worried, starting to be alarmed. Now she expresses herself.)*

VERONICA. Waaaaaaaaaaaaaaa! Waaaaaaaaaaaaaaaaaaaa! *(Her cries are those of an unhappy baby; momentarily she switches to adult self, and looks around her, horrified.)* Oh my God! Where am I? Oh Lord. *(Back to crying.)* Waaaaaaaaaaaaaa!

MOTHER 2. Shut up! God, it's so ugly when it cries. *(To the baby.)* You're ugly!

VERONICA. *(Adult for a sec.)* Oh, God, what is this? Do they have a dog, I wonder? *(Baby again.)* Waaaaaaaaaaaaa!

MOTHER 2. Shut up! *(To husband.)* Where's Spot the wonder

22

dog, I want him to meet baby.

VERONICA. *(As adult.)* Oh good! *(As baby, happy.)* Ga ga, ga ga.

FATHER 2. I shot the dog this morning. *(Veronica looks a bit appalled, as well as worried — how does she get out of here?)*

MOTHER 2. Oh, so that's what that noise was. I thought you farted. *(Laughs at her joke, but then:)* How come you shot the dog?

FATHER 2. It annoyed me.

VERONICA. *(Adult.)* Oh Lord. How do I get out of this? *(Baby.)* Waaaaaaaaaaaaaa!

MOTHER 2. God, it's such a noisy baby. Do you think it's defective?

FATHER 2. Well, it came out your fat ass, it's bound to be defective.

MOTHER 2. I need a joint. Do you think the baby can inhale? Maybe that'll stop it from crying. You want some pot, baby? That shut you up?

VERONICA. *(Adult, thinking, worried.)* No dog. No escape. Pot. Okay. *(Baby, nods.)* Ahhh, ga ga. *(Lights dim down briefly, come back up. To signify time passing.)*

Scene 7

Veronica is now very much a five-year-old girl. Kind of normal, vulnerable. But also unhappy, a little "dead." She doesn't seem to have access to her adult "soul self" anymore. She is no longer in the tub/bassinet, she's seated on a chair. Mother 2 and Father 2 are still there, though it's five years later for them too. Father 2 seems out of it.

MOTHER 2. Hey, Ginny. You want another piece of pie?

VERONICA. Okay.

MOTHER 2. Wipe your mouth, you look like a pig.

VERONICA. Am I pretty?

MOTHER 2. Didn't I just call you a pig?

VERONICA. Yes.

MOTHER 2. So don't ask dumb questions.

VERONICA. I'm hungry.

MOTHER 2. So eat another piece of pie, I told you to. You're so fat already, it don't matter what you eat.

VERONICA. Will I ever go to school?

MOTHER 2. Stop asking about school. We're doin' home schooling with you, so you can learn real values. *(To Father 2.)* You're awful quiet today.

FATHER 2. That's because I'm overdosing. *(Falls down dead.)*

MOTHER 2. Oh fuck. You jerk. Leaving me alone. Oh fuck. I need to shoot up. Finish your pie, Ginny.

VERONICA. *(Worried.)* Don't take an overdose.

MOTHER 2. I know what I'm doin'. Give me ten minutes to get high first, and then call an ambulance for him. And finish your pie. *(Exits, muttering.)* Fuckin' useless husband. *(Veronica/Ginny looks around, kind of lost.)*

VERONICA. Dad? You dead? I'm gonna call the ambulance, but Mom said to wait ten minutes, she wants to get high. *(Looks around, more sense of panic, being lost.)* Maybe I better have two pieces of pie.

(Lights dim. Noise, various noises — trucks, horns, trucks backing up beep-beep-beep. They're not necessarily in a city — though they may be. It's just there are noises, unpleasant ones. It's "time passing" noises. The noises lessen, and we hear voices in the dark.)

MOTHER 2. *(Voice.)* What's seven times seven?

GINNY. *(Voice.)* I don't know.

MOTHER 2. Well, think, idiot.

GINNY. Fifty-six.

MOTHER 2. No! *(Slap sound.)*

GINNY. Ow!

MOTHER 2. Forty-nine, forty-nine … I give up, two years of home schooling is killin' me, you're going to public school, how do ya like that?

GINNY. I'd like it fine. *(Slap sound.)* Ow!

MOTHER 2. Don't be fresh!

GINNY. I wasn't! *(Sound of a big slap.)* OW!

Scene 8

A school room. Lights up on a teacher. She sits at a desk. There are two chairs by the desk. The teacher is a black woman, sympathetic, intelligent. Mother 2 and Veronica/Ginny come in.

TEACHER. Ah, you must be Mrs. Fortunata. I'm afraid I'm running late, I can't give you as much time as I planned, the previous student had a nosebleed.

MOTHER 2. *(Curious.)* Did ya punch him?

TEACHER. *(Slightly taken aback.)* No, it was just a nosebleed. But I hadn't allotted time for it, and now I've fallen behind. Sorry. *(Realizes she hasn't said hi to Ginny.)* Hello, Virginia, how are you today? *(Ginny shrugs; to Mother.)* And thank you so much for coming.

MOTHER 2. Sure.

TEACHER. Mrs. Fortunata, I wanted to talk to you because Virginia seems kind of lost in school.

MOTHER 2. *(To Veronica/Ginny, immediately "at" her.)* What did I tell you about being lost? Huh? What did I say?

VERONICA. I don't know. You say a lot of things.

MOTHER 2. Well, pay attention to what I say. *(To teacher.)* She don't listen to what I say.

TEACHER. *(Slightly considers correcting her grammar, decides not to.)* Uh-huh. Well, she's not learning at the seventh-grade level.

MOTHER 2. *(Looking at Ginny during the above comment.)* Ginny, your mind is wandering, stop it. *(Mother 2 snaps her fingers. Veronica looks over at her mother, blankly.)* Pay attention! *(Pinches Veronica/Ginny.)*

VERONICA. Ow!

MOTHER 2. *(To teacher.)* Go ahead. You have about six seconds she'll keep listening.

TEACHER. *(Bit disoriented by the mother.)* Okay. As I said, I'm concerned about Virginia. She's failing most of her subjects.

MOTHER 2. *(To Ginny.)* Why can't you learn anything? You're useless. *(Swats her on the head.)*

TEACHER. Uh … no hitting please. Lord, I don't have time to solve this.

MOTHER 2. What?

TEACHER. Nothing. Just we have a "no hitting" policy.

MOTHER 2. I don't believe that socialist crap you can't hit your kids. *(To Veronica.)* You don't do better in school, and I'm yankin' you outta here, and we're doin' home schooling again. How'd you like that?

VERONICA. You don't know nothin'.

MOTHER 2. You have respect for your mother, you fat pig. *(To teacher.)* You see what I have to go through with her?

VERONICA. You're right, I'm useless.

MOTHER 2. *(Makes a fist.)* How'd you like a bloody nose, you keep talkin' back to me?

TEACHER. STOP IT, STOP IT!

MOTHER 2. What?

TEACHER. This is not acceptable behavior.

MOTHER 2. What isn't?

TEACHER. Mrs. Fortunata, I'd like to speak to you *without* Virginia being here for a moment.

MOTHER 2. Anything you wanna say to me, just say it. She can hear it.

TEACHER. *(Pause, decides to go ahead.)* Mrs. Fortunata, I'm … upset how you speak to your daughter.

MOTHER 2. I'm the mother, I gotta correct her. She's constantly failing, what, I'm supposed to praise her for that? *(To Ginny, with a mocking voice.)* Oh, Ginny, you're so good! You're dumb and you're fat, but it's fun to watch you eat twenty doughnuts at a time, and maybe you can grow up and be a elephant in the circus. Ginny's great, Ginny's great!

VERONICA. I want to take an overdose like Daddy did.

MOTHER 2. You're too young for hard drugs.

TEACHER. STOP IT, STOP IT!

MOTHER 2. Stop telling me to stop it. You stop it!

TEACHER. Virginia can't survive if you tell her she's worthless.

MOTHER 2. *(To Ginny.)* Did I call you worthless?

VERONICA. You did yesterday!

MOTHER 2. I'm not talking about yesterday.

TEACHER. STOP! Look, I'm not a psychologist, but maybe the school can come up with money to send you both for family counseling. I'm sorry, I have to move on to the next patient now … I mean parent.

MOTHER 2. *(Fed up, gets up to go.)* Counseling! You go to counseling, I'm going to the liquor store. Come on, Ginny, let's get you an ice cream cone. *(Mother 2 takes Veronica/Ginny off. The teacher looks exhausted, she holds her head in her hands, or shudders, or does something to deal with bad energy.)*

TEACHER. Oh, Lord. *(Lights dim as the teacher exits.)*

Scene 9

Sounds of a playground. A sleazy man enters into the playground. Played by same actor who was Father 1 and Father 2. Moustache, lanky, loose. Wears black jeans, black T-shirt, maybe leather jacket. Sleazy, but a bit sexy too.

SLEAZY MAN. *(Has a British accent of some sort; speaks to a child who is presumably walking by.)* Hey, luv. Want some smoke? Special sale today, come on, honey. *(Sleazy man looks disappointed, looks after where the child presumably exited. Enter Veronica/Ginny, drinking a diet soda.)* Hey, Ginny.

VERONICA. Hello, Stanley.

SLEAZY MAN. You got that "wantin' it" look in your eye. I told you, hun, you gotta have money. I'm not a charity organization.

VERONICA. I got money today. For my birthday.

SLEAZY MAN. Oh, how old are you?

VERONICA. I'm thirteen.

SLEAZY MAN. That's a good age. Soon you can have your own baby and ruin her life. That's a good revenge, huh?

VERONICA. Where in England are you from?

SLEAZY MAN. Liverpool.

VERONICA. I like English accents. In school they showed us this movie from years and years ago called *My Fair Lady*, and Rex Harrison taught Audrey Hepburn how to talk good. *(Corrects herself.)* To talk well.

SLEAZY MAN. Yeah, I saw that once. Very long movie.

VERONICA. You remind me of Rex Harrison somehow.

SLEAZY MAN. Do I? It must be me charm. So how much money you got today?

VERONICA. Fifty.

SLEAZY MAN. Oh, you're doing well.

VERONICA. I got ten for my birthday, and I got forty more nobody knows about.

SLEAZY MAN. Atta girl. I can sell you a good party for fifty.

VERONICA. Do you have some of those pills you talked about? That make you spacey and happy?

SLEAZY MAN. I sure do, sweet cakes. You can have three for fifty.

VERONICA. Three? *(It seems a small number to her.)*

SLEAZY MAN. They're really good.

VERONICA. Okay.

SLEAZY MAN. But spread 'em out, don't take 'em all at once or you won't wake up.

VERONICA. Three would do that?

SLEAZY MAN. If you don't spread 'em out.

VERONICA. Alright, I'll spread 'em out. *(She hands him the money; he gives her a little packet, pretending he's not doing a transaction, looking around or something.)*

SLEAZY MAN. *(Sings to himself, while they do the above exchange.)*
> London Bridge is falling down,
> Falling down, falling down,
> London Bridge is …

(Jumps to end of melody.) … my fair lady. *(Done with selling, ready to move on.)* Well, you have a nice party, Virginia.

VERONICA. Thanks. *(Sleazy man exits.)*

(Veronica looks around, takes a pill, drinks from diet soda. A thought now crosses her mind. Makes a decision. Takes a second pill. Pauses. Takes a third pill.)

Happy birthday, Virginia.

(Lights dim. Emergency sounds, ambulance, flashing lights. Then whooshing noise, then wind, then ocean sounds. Final whoosh and —)

Scene 10

Veronica is back in the bardo. She's a bit shell-shocked.

VERONICA. Oh God. *(Enter Maryamma.)*

MARYAMMA. *(Disapproving, maybe angry.)* I see you're back.

VERONICA. That was horrible! How could you do that to me? I had no chance in that situation, that was pure hell.

MARYAMMA. No one did it to you, Miss Witherspoon. Your soul makes the choice of the life that will teach you the lesson you need to learn.

VERONICA. What lesson was that? Life is hell? I already knew that.

MARYAMMA. I can't explain it to you fully. It's not punishment, but it's karma, we have to learn. And you keep killing yourself, that doesn't make good karma. You don't get ahead with suicide.

VERONICA. Next time you try to reincarnate me, I'm going to be able to stop it again. I know I will.

MARYAMMA. Well. You're very willful. We've all noted it.

VERONICA. I mean what else could I have done with that life?

MARYAMMA. I don't know. You could have tried to befriend the teacher.

VERONICA. What good would that have done?

MARYAMMA. *(Sharp.)* Well, I don't know. You didn't try it.

VERONICA. I was depressed. I was hyperglycemic. I was on various drugs.

MARYAMMA. I admit. It was a very difficult life. For your next life …

VERONICA. Don't finish that sentence. I need to recuperate after that life. *(Getting upset.)* Did you ever see *Stop the World I Want to Get Off*? That musical with Anthony Newley, I think Rex and I saw it together — and I *was* married to him, don't tell me I knew him when he was a coal miner in some previous century — anyway that musical's title was prescient, wasn't it? Who thought Anthony Newley knew anything? Oddest singer I ever heard, but he was on to something. Stop the world, stop the bardo, I want off. Don't send me back for more suffering. What's the matter with you?

MARYAMMA. *(Softer, sympathetic to her upset.)* Suffering and life

29

are mysteries, Miss Witherspoon. We can't choose to escape from them. They are inescapable.

VERONICA. *(Pause; stares at her; cold.)* May I see St. Peter please?

MARYAMMA. *(Uncertain pause; then:)* I'll see what I can do. *(Maryamma exits.)*

VERONICA. *(Calling after her.)* And I don't want him to look like E.T. either! I want him in a beard and a staff and a robe. I don't want any "modern interpretations" of him, for God's sake. *(Veronica is pent up, upset. She shakes her arms and whole body, as if to "shake off" the experience of the last life. She looks out to the audience.)* Well, I think I made a point with her. All this repeating of life after life. Christianity taught me one life, one roll of the dice, and it's heaven, hell or purgatory, but it's clear and simple. And it's over.

So St. Peter can set this straight, I hope. Because for most of my lives I was a Christian, so I am expecting heaven or purgatory.

I don't want hell, of course, but after all I wasn't Hitler, I may have my quirks, but really purgatory should be the appropriate place for me, I believe. That's just that place where you can't see God for eons and eons 'cause you weren't perfect, and I don't know, it may be unpleasant, but I don't think they torture you there or anything. Maybe you only eat bread or water. Maybe it's like prison. But not Spanish Inquisition prison —that would be more like hell — it's just "prison" prison.

Here I am longing for purgatory. Strange, I actually thought the afterlife would be nothing … you know, like life is a television set with horrible things on it, but then you die and the television set is just unplugged. Nothing going in, nothing going out. I want to be unplugged!

I can't stand the idea that this just goes on forever. Or if not forever, until you learn one hundred and two fucking lessons. Who came up with that idea? The American Federation of Teachers? *(Whoosh sound begins. She holds onto her chair.)* Oh my God, another life is starting. NO! I'm waiting to see St. Peter, I'm not available for another life right now. I'm on hold. I can't go, I won't go. *(Whoosh stops.)* Good. My force of will is working again. *(Whoosh starts again.)* AAAAAAggggggghhhhh! NO NO NO NO NO NO NO NO! *(Whoosh stops again.)* Thank God.

I think I did stop it. Just like those other times. My little brake system. Stubbornness is a wonderful thing.

Now if only my brain will let up. I don't see why Jewish people and Jean Paul Sartre get to be in some general anesthesia state, and

I get to remember things and fret and worry, and my brain goes on and on, and I just don't like it. It's not fair. *(Thinking of other people who get this state.)* Albert Camus, Simone Signoret probably.

How am I to learn "lessons" anyway if they don't tell me what they are, and if I can't really remember the past lives when I'm down there. And what lessons am I supposed to learn? *(Calling.)* Maryamma! I'm still waiting for St. Peter. Are you bringing him? I really am a Christian. Tell him that!

(To self or audience.) Though that's not really true. I have a problem with the crucifixion. I didn't used to, I didn't used to think about it ... but the meaning of it has become ... "odd" to me. I mean, it starts with Adam and Eve, eating the apple ... which is disobedient, and God goes *ballistic* — creates death and suffering, and punishes *everybody* by giving them original sin, which keeps them out of heaven forever.

But after a while God cools down a bit. And now He feels bad no one can get into heaven. So then he goes, "I know I know, I'll send down my only son to be tortured and die." And we are taught that somehow this sacrifice will expiate our sins. "Atone for."

So when I was seven, I believed that.

But when I was twenty-seven, I got to thinking about sacrifice, and how in the Old Testament God seems to require animal sacrifices ... "Kill an animal for me, so I know you love me." Which seems a bit odd, why does he find it pleasing that we kill animals for him?

And then he almost moved up to human sacrifice when he told Abraham to kill his son Isaac ... but then God relented and said, "No, no — you can just kill an animal for me, I was testing you."

But then later God himself does what he stopped Abraham from doing — he lets his only begotten son die so that our sins can be atoned for.

But what about forgiveness *without* killing an animal? Or a person? Or your son? I don't understand it, it doesn't make sense.

Imagine if your child did something really, really bad, and you said, "Okay I'm going to forgive you, but we're going to have to kill your sister first."

I mean, do you understand psychologically what my problem is with the crucifixion?

I bet this isn't a popular thought I'm expressing, but that's how it strikes me now. And why I can't really call myself a Christian. *(Frowns, realizes:)* Oh, except I'm waiting for St. Peter. No, I *do* believe in the crucifixion. I believe it all! *(Calls off after Maryamma again.)* Maryamma! I'm still waiting for St. Peter! I'm a Christian!

Oh God, I bet St. Peter won't talk to me. I'm stuck in this netherworld with this lady in a sari. *(Sings briefly:)* Who's sari now? *(Depressed.)* Pretty good joke, huh?

I'm feeling tired. I'm afraid they're gonna send me back, like some soldier sent back to the front over and over and over. Some of them kill themselves rather than stay there ... that's what I did. But it doesn't stop it. *Oh God, suicide isn't an out anymore, it's just a doorway to another awful life!*

Oh, that last life. Poor little Ginny, there wasn't any hope for her. And even though she was fat, I could tell she was going to live till ninety or something, suffering through an endless succession of tedious days and tedious nights ... that's a phrase from *Uncle Vanya*, or rather a translation of it, the real play's in Russian, I don't know the Russian, I saw Rex in *Uncle Vanya*, he was very good. Oh God, I'm getting sleepy ... my force of will is feeling weak ... uh-oh ... Maryamma! St. Peter! ... *(Whoosh sounds. Wind.)* Not now, I'm busy, come back later. Go away. Maryamma! ... St. Peter! *(Lights off of Veronica. The sound of returning to earth continues.)*

Scene 11

Lights up. We're in a grassy spot. A doghouse might be nearby. Veronica is standing, looking off. A man in jeans and a sports shirt comes in, friendly. He is played by same actor who played the Father 1 and Father 2.

MAN. Here, boy. Come here.

(At the sound of his voice, Veronica barks happily and runs up to him, thrilled to see him. She is, obviously, a dog. Perhaps a golden retriever. It might be best if the actress played the dog standing, rather than getting on all fours. But otherwise she should do her best to seem like a dog.)

VERONICA. *(Barks happily.)* Rrrrrrffff rrrrrrrrfff rrrrrrrrrrrfff!

MAN. That's a good boy. Go get the ball! *(He throws a ball out. Veronica runs after it, and puts the ball in her mouth. With her hand, maybe, she indicates a wagging tail — puts hand behind her back near her buttocks and moves it happily back and forth. She runs back to the man. In this life, the dog is really, really happy. Veronica's adult doesn't break through. Just a happy life, primarily.)*

Good boy! Now give me the ball. Lonnie, come on, give it to me. *(The man tries to take the ball from her mouth, but she playfully resists for a while. He acts like he's going to give up and go away, and then she abruptly drops the ball. He picks the ball up again, and she then looks super-attentive, and does the hand-wagging-the-tail thing like mad. Pants, excited. The man prepares to throw it out again.)*

Okay, good boy, get it now! *(Man throws the ball again. Veronica runs after it, panting happily. She gets it in her mouth and runs back to him.)*

Good boy. You want a treat? *(Veronica is thrilled out of her mind. Wags tail, looks ecstatic. Man gives imaginary treat and Veronica indicates she's chewing it up, very happy.)*

Good boy. Now, go to your bed for a while, I have to go to work. *(Veronica crestfallen ... she knows he's leaving, doesn't want him to go. BIG mood change.)*

VERONICA. *(Whimpers slightly.)* Errrrrrrrrr ... errrrrrrr ...

MAN. I know. But I'll be back later. I have to go to work. You be a good dog. That's right, Lonnie. Good boy. *(The man pats her on the head, then exits.)*

(Veronica looks sad. Is very still. Just stares. Then looks around, not too interested in anything. Then she has some sort of happy thought. It makes her wag her tail like mad, her face lights up, very, very happy. It makes her pant happily too. Then the thought passes, and she returns to silence and just staring again. She stays that way a few beats. Time passes. Man comes back.)

I'm back. I know I'm later than usual but ... *(At the sound of his returning voice Veronica is thrilled out of her mind, wags her tail again, and rushes over to him, barking happily.)*

VERONICA. Rrrrrrf, rrrrrrrf, rrrrrrrrf! Rrrrrrf, rrrrrrrf, rrrrrrrrf!

MAN. Good boy. You're so good. If I was late for my girlfriend, she'd just go, where were you? Why didn't you call? Dogs are so good. Good boy, good boy. Wanna go for a run? *(Veronica pants and jumps up and down, tail wagging.)* Good boy! That's a good boy!

(The man and Veronica run off happily, to the park. Lights dim, the grassy scene and the doghouse disappear.)

Scene 12

We are suddenly back in the bardo. Maryamma is there. Veronica enters, looking happy.

VERONICA. Oh, I feel refreshed after that.
MARYAMMA. Yes, your aura is a little less tweedy.
VERONICA. I can't remember much of it, actually. But it was nice.
MARYAMMA. What do you remember?
VERONICA. Ummm ... smells. Running in the park. Being patted on the head. Good God, was I a dog?
MARYAMMA. Yes.
VERONICA. Oh. Well, I liked it. I think I liked it more than any of the human incarnations. I don't remember worrying and thinking ahead. I just seemed happy in the present. I don't remember dying, how did I die?
MARYAMMA. Well, let me show you.

(Maryamma and Veronica are on one part of the stage. The lighting changes on another part of the stage, and is on earth, somewhere near the park the man and the dog went. The man comes on happy, with energy.)

MAN. Good boy! Be careful of the cars. That's a good boy. *(Sound of a tire screeching, terrible car crash.)* Oh no! Lonnie! *(The man is in shock, upset.)*

(Enter Mother 1 from the first baby scene. Dressed either the same, or very recognizable from that earlier scene. She runs in, also upset.)

MOTHER 1. I'm so sorry!
MAN. You killed my dog.
MOTHER 1. It was my son actually. I was following in my car.

MAN. Following him?

MOTHER 1. Well, he's only sixteen and he doesn't have his license and he was drunk and I couldn't stop him from driving ... his father and I are terrible at discipline. It's really our fault, I imagine. Would you be willing not to call the police? I'll get you another dog. I'll pay you.

MAN. Pay me? Not to report this. Are you crazy?

MOTHER 1. Oh please, it will hurt his record if he's been driving drunk at sixteen without a license.

MAN. It's not just my dog. He killed two people.

MOTHER 1. He did? (*Man points offstage. Mother 1 looks offstage, gasps.*) Oh my God. I didn't see them. Oh dear. How much money can I give you to buy your silence? Would ten thousand dollars work?

MAN. I'm sorry. I have to call the police. Your son is a menace.

MOTHER 1. It's not his fault! It's our fault. We spoiled him. He's our second child, and our first one was killed by our dog, and we felt such guilt ...

(*Veronica "gets" it now, who hit her in the car, and she doesn't care for it. Looks over at Maryamma, who tries not to give too much of a response.*)

MAN. Killed by your dog?

MOTHER 1. Oh, that's not why our son hit your dog, he likes dogs, I'm the one who has mixed feelings about them, but I'd never hit one with a car, I just would be more stringent about leaving it alone with a baby. But, you see, we spoiled him ... and this will ruin his life if the police get called. The two people are already dead, it won't help them to punish my son.

MAN. I'm going to find a phone right now. (*Exits with purpose, and also to get away from her.*)

MOTHER 1. (*Calls after him.*) Oh, you're a heartless person ... (*Calls in the direction of where the car crash was.*) Run for the hills, Timmy! Mummy and Daddy will find you later. Run, darling. No, leave the vodka bottle behind, dear. We love you! Oh God. I need a drink. (*Mother 1 walks or runs in the direction of Timmy, very discouraged.*)

(*The "on earth" lighting goes away, and we're back in the bardo. Maryamma is looking at Veronica, who looks annoyed.*)

MARYAMMA. Any comments?

VERONICA. I suppose you want me to feel guilty. It's not my fault how they brought up their son. They've clearly done a bad job.

MARYAMMA. I'm not interested in guilt. I'm interested if you can *learn any lessons* from your experiences and from their repercussions.

VERONICA. You and these lessons. Alright — I shouldn't have urged that dog to kill me when I was two weeks old, that was suicide which apparently is frowned upon; and what d'ya know, lo and behold, in a stunning ironic twist, when I reincarnate as a dog, I am killed by the messed-up and tragic son that I created by inviting that earlier dog to end my life in that quick and violent manner. So the lesson is … I'm bad, I'm bad, kick me when I'm down, I'm bad.

MARYAMMA. The lesson is never I am bad. At our core we are not bad. The lesson can be: I should not commit suicide. It could be: I must be aware my actions have an impact on other people.

VERONICA. Yes, yes, fine. Well, great, I thought I had a good time as a dog, and now it turns out it was just a set-up to make me feel crummy and punished.

MARYAMMA. You set yourself up, that's one of the lessons.

VERONICA. If you say the word "lesson" one more time, I will have to sit on your chest and hold my hand over your mouth to prevent any more comments from you.

MARYAMMA. *(Laughs.)* Oh, you are a tough nut to crack, Miss Witherspoon. Alright, let's forget about the drunk sixteen-year-old for now … and you're partially right, of course, your actions impacted the situation but they made their own choices.

VERONICA. Well, thank you!

MARYAMMA. But you liked being a dog. Tell me about it.

VERONICA. It was relaxing. I was happy most of the time. I liked sniffing things in the grass. I liked running after the ball. I felt very much in the present.

MARYAMMA. Being in the present. That is a very good les … *(Stops herself from saying "lesson.")* … enlightenment to comprehend. Notice I didn't use the "L" word.

VERONICA. Yes. And I so appreciate it.

MARYAMMA. You're welcome.

VERONICA. What happened to St. Peter?

MARYAMMA. I couldn't find him. But I put in a request. Rest for a while. Have some ginger tea. I'll be back later. *(Exits.)*

VERONICA. Where do I get the ginger tea? *(No answer.)* Typical. Oh well. Let me rest a minute. *(She sits back in her chair, tired. She closes her eyes. Then there is a voice — a soothing, male voice. Very soothing. Veronica opens her eyes, listens.)*

VOICE. Welcome to the General Anesthesia Afterlife, available for Jewish people and Albert Camus and Jean-Paul Sartre. Think of nothing. Think of nothing. Nothingness. Blankness.

VERONICA. Oh, thank goodness.

VOICE. Nothing. Nothingness. Blankness.

VERONICA. Oh, this is lovely. *(Closes her eyes in pleasure; keeps them closed.)*

VOICE. Nothing. No thing. The absence of color. The absence of sound. Rest in the quiet of nothing. Negative numbers. Minus one. Minus two. Minus three. Minus one hundred thousand seven hundred and thirty-three. Blank. Blank. Blank. Blunk. Blenk. You could be getting a colonoscopy, and you wouldn't even be aware. Blank. Blunk. Blenk. Blink. Blink of an eye, and there's nothing. Nothing. Absence of consciousness. Forgetting. No memory. No thoughts. Blankness. *(Right after the voice says "you wouldn't even be aware" in his recitation above, things start happening on the stage.)*

Scene 13

Suddenly Mother 2 and Father 2 are back, the trailer trash parents of Ginny. Mother 2 and Father 2 are in the same position they were in the first trailer trash scene, but the bassinet isn't there, though they look at the spot where it was as if it is still there. Even if there was much of a set for the trailer trash family, it may not all return at this time. Veronica stays seated, seemingly asleep. Her face begins to show discomfort. As the male voice fades away, she can register that something upsetting is impinging on her consciousness when she hears Mother 2 and Father 2's voices.

MOTHER 2. Hey, baby. Gee, it's kind of a fat baby, isn't it?

FATHER 2. Yeah, it's gonna have your fat ass. *(Veronica opens her eyes, very disturbed.)*

MOTHER 2. Shut up. It's gonna have your greasy hair and damaged brain cells.

FATHER 2. Yeah, well, I had fun damaging them.

MOTHER 2. Good for you. Why isn't the baby responding? Is it dead? Hey, fat-ass! You dead?

VERONICA. Oh God. I've done this one.

(From here the familiar scene of Mother 2 and Father 2 seems to skip ahead, like a record skipping, or like a DVD fast-forwarding where you see a snippet of something and then it jumps ahead to a later snippet. Mother 2 and Father 2 should recreate their previous staging, but when lines seem to jump ahead to later in a scene, their physical transitions can be jerky and abrupt. Often times they say parts of a sentence, not the whole sentence. It should all be fast. And there probably should be odd sounds in the background, a mechanical noise that somehow adds to the feeling that this isn't "normal" life, but is moving ahead in snippets.)

FATHER 2. I shot the dog.

MOTHER 2. Is the baby defective?

FATHER 2. Well, it came out your fat ass.

MOTHER 2. Hey, Ginny. Hey, Ginny! *(This calling of her name makes Veronica enter the scene as a participant — though she doesn't leave her chair, she doesn't enter into their physical space. But she re-becomes little Ginny living this past life, though still seated in her bardo chair.)* Wipe your mouth, you look like a pig.

VERONICA. Am I pretty?

MOTHER 2. … pig.

VERONICA. … hungry.

MOTHER 2. We're doin' home schoolin'.

FATHER 2. I'm overdosing. *(Falls down dead.)*

MOTHER 2. Oh fuck.

VERONICA. Dad? You dead?

MOTHER 2. What's seven times seven?

VERONICA. Fifty-six. *(Mother 2 slaps the air where Ginny would be; we hear a slap sound.)* Ow!

MOTHER 2. You're going to public school.

VERONICA. Fine. *(Mother 2 slaps her again.)* Ow! *(The teacher arrives. Her desk and chair should arrive back too.)*

TEACHER. … must be Mrs. Fortunata.

MOTHER 2. Did ya punch him?

TEACHER. Virginia seems lost.

MOTHER 2. She don't listen. *(Swats her on the head. Again, it's by hitting the air where she would've been.)*

38

VERONICA. Ow!

TEACHER. … no hitting!

MOTHER 2. … socialist crap … hit your kids.

VERONICA. … *(You.)* don't know nothin'.

MOTHER 2. Respect … fat pig.

TEACHER. STOP IT, STOP IT!

VERONICA. … overdose like Daddy.

MOTHER 2. Too young.

TEACHER. STOP IT, STOP IT!

MOTHER 2. You stop it!

TEACHER. Counseling!

MOTHER 2. Liquor store! Come on … ice cream!

TEACHER. Lord. *(Mother 2 exits, as if she is taking Veronica/Ginny off with her. The teacher looks exhausted. Sounds of playground, as happened in previous scene with the cockney drug dealer. We hear the sound of the drug dealer singing "London Bridge is Falling Down," though it's a bit distant, a bit distorted. Veronica looks up at the sound of his song. She remembers what happened after he left her in the playground. Veronica stands and crosses into the school space with the teacher.)*

Scene 14

Veronica has become Ginny again. The skipping ahead now stops. And background noise stops as well.

VERONICA. 'Scuse me.

TEACHER. Virginia. I … uh … have been thinking of you since our meeting with your mother.

VERONICA. I got some money for my birthday, and I bought some pills. You know, happy pills. But then I didn't use them.

TEACHER. *(Not sure what to say.)* All right.

VERONICA. I saw this old, old movie about Liza Doolittle and she meets Professor Higgins, and I didn't like him, there's something that grosses me out about him, I think he's mean, and selfish and he don't really care about Liza although at the end she comes back to him but then he just wants her to hand him his slippers like

39

she's the maid or something. But he does teach her things. And her life gets better.

TEACHER. *My Fair Lady*. You saw *My Fair Lady*.

VERONICA. Yes, and I saw her life got better, and she dressed better and she talked better. And I wondered if you could teach me. *(Suddenly afraid there's no way the teacher will say yes.)* You're probably too busy. But I wondered if maybe you weren't.

TEACHER. *(Looks at her closely; makes decision.)* I'd like to teach you. I'd need you to work hard. But if you worked hard, I'd work hard with you. *(Veronica/Ginny is shocked she got a yes to her question. And deeply grateful. It doesn't seem possible in this world.)*

VERONICA. *(Softly.)* Wow. Thank you. *(Lights dim and come up again. Or the lights on them change substantially. Something to indicate passage of time.)*

Scene 15

The classroom. A few weeks later.

TEACHER. *(Reciting as a lesson.)* In Hartford, Hereford and Hampshire, hurricanes hardly ever happen.

VERONICA. But hurricanes are happening more now. And tornados. And meteorites.

TEACHER. Yes, I guess that's true. The weather has been changing. *(Teaching again.)* The rain in Spain stays mainly in the plain.

VERONICA. Will that be on the SATs?

TEACHER. Well, this is about speaking.

VERONICA. Oh. The rine in Spine sties minely on the pline.

TEACHER. No, Ginny. Plain.

VERONICA. I know, I'm pretending to be cockney.

TEACHER. Oh. *(She laughs; she hadn't gotten it; now she recites again, with energy:)* Sister Susie's sewing shirts for soldiers. Such skill at sewing shirts my shy young sister Susie shows. Some soldiers write epistles, say they'd sooner sleep on thistles than the soft and saucy shirts for soldiers sister Susie sews.

VERONICA. What?

TEACHER. *(As if this is teaching too, but her voice starts to fade as it goes on, and she begins to exit, still speaking.)* Negative numbers. Minus one. Minus two. Minus three. Minus four. Minus one hundred thousand seven hundred and thirty-three. Minus one hundred thousand seven hundred and thirty-four. *(Maybe the soothing man's voice joins the teacher's voice as she's exiting. Or not. In any case, the lights dim down and the teacher exits. Veronica leaves the school area, and goes to a different area, defined tightly by light.)*

Scene 16

Mother 2 comes into the space, very much the worse for wear. She looks like she's gone back to using drugs, her hair is messy, and she's a little non-distinct, like a drunk who makes her points emphatically but messily. From their behavior together, we assume they are in their house or trailer. Veronica/Ginny is either practicing something from a book she's holding — moving her mouth, trying to memorize it for an assignment; or she's just doing stetching exercises, trying to ignore her mother. As the scene goes on, we realize Veronica/Ginny is two to three years older. She's a bit more sure of herself.

MOTHER 2. I don't want you seeing that teacher anymore. She's filling your head with lies. You're gonna fail, and I don't want you to forget it.
VERONICA. Why don't you take an overdose and die?
MOTHER 2. The Bible says, "Honor your parents." Did I kill you? Did I abort you? Did I pour scalding water on your private parts? Well, did I?
VERONICA. No.
MOTHER 2. And can you say thank you?
VERONICA. Thank you for not pouring scalding water on my private parts. *(A large metal thing suddenly falls from the sky — as happened in the beginning of the play. Both Veronica and Mother 2 scream.)*
MOTHER 2 and VERONICA. Aaaaaaaaaaaaghhh!
MOTHER 2. Damn it! The sky is falling, the sky is falling!
VERONICA. It's one of those meteorites.

MOTHER 2. It's not a piece of plane or something?

VERONICA. No.

MOTHER 2. Remember when the toilet from that plane dropped down and killed the postman?

VERONICA. Well, it doesn't look like a toilet, does it? *(Sound of terrible wind.)*

MOTHER 2. Uh-oh. Another torpedo.

VERONICA. Tornado, not torpedo.

MOTHER 2. Don't talk back.

VERONICA. Didn't we have a hurricane yesterday? What's the matter with the weather?

MOTHER 2. I don't know, something about the air. Go to the cellar.

VERONICA. We don't have a cellar.

MOTHER 2. Well, get away from the window then. *(Terrible wind. We hear the sudden sound of a glass window breaking. Lights go out totally, briefly. Maybe Mother 2 screams. Lots of noise. It sounds like a scary storm. Wind stops. Quiet. Lights come back up.*

Scene 17

Lights focus back on the school area. There is a banner: "Congratulations, Graduates." We see Veronica standing, waiting to speak. The teacher is also onstage, wearing a corsage, standing off to the side and watching Veronica proudly. Mother 2 is not there.

VERONICA. I am so proud to be graduating today. I never thought I would be chosen as the commencement speaker. In Hartford, Hereford and Hampshire, hurricanes hardly ever happen. That's from a movie with Rex Harrison back many years ago. *(Lights go out. Or for theatre purposes, they greatly dim.)*

Oh dear. It's hard to give a commencement speech in the dark. But of course the weather is so changeable from minute to minute, the lights are always going out. But then you know that. You're sitting in the dark as well. But we can get used to so many things. *(The lights suddenly come up to normal, bright levels, as if elec-*

tricity has been restored. There's a little buzz when it comes back on.)

Oh, that's good. Now I can see you. I am so grateful to my teacher Mrs. Donaldson. She is the mother I never had. *(Mother 2, still looking a wreck, briefly juts her head in from the side of the stage. She shouts in Ginny's direction:)*

MOTHER 2. I am your mother! *(Promptly disappears off again.)*

VERONICA. *(Shouting after her in full, expressed fury.)* SHUT UP, YOU DRUG-ADDICTED, SADISTIC, SUBHUMAN PIECE OF SHIT! *(Shocked at herself, and abashed; to audience.)* I'm so sorry! That's not part of my commencement address. *(Looks back at the teacher, who indicates not to worry, just go on.)*

We're living in a scary world. Volatile, turbulent. Small chunks of meteorites keep braining us on the head. Sometimes we have tornadoes five days in a row. Then there will be a massive snowstorm in July. Drought in some states, while others receive seven inches of rain in two hours and become flooded. The government says they must do further study before anything can be done. *(The sound of a rumble begins.)*

Uh-oh. Another earthquake. Hold onto your seats and hope the ceiling doesn't fall. *(Lights go dim again.)*

There they go again. *(Sound of earthquake noises. Alarming. Veronica tries to speak over it.)*

Everyone remain calm. It's probably just a small one. Say your mantras. Blankness. The absence of color. The absence of sound. Negative numbers. Minus one. Minus two. Minus three. Minus one hundred thousand seven hundred and thirty-three. Blank. Blank. Blink of an eye, and then nothing. Forgetting. No memory. No thoughts. Blankness. *(The lights fade to black during the above. The teacher exits. Veronica, while saying the mantra words, starts making her way to her chair in the bardo. The sounds crescendo as the lights go to black.)*

Scene 18

The terrible sounds stop. Lights come up. Back in the bardo. Veronica is seated on her chair. Her eyes are closed. She opens them. Maryamma is standing over her.

MARYAMMA. Miss Witherspoon, you've been asleep for several decades. How are you feeling?

VERONICA. Decades? Good Lord. Well, I feel very rested. Though I also feel sort of stirred up.

MARYAMMA. I relented. I decided your spirit needed to replenish itself, and so we let you have the afterlife you had requested.

VERONICA. You mean the anesthesia afterlife. But I'm confused. I seemed to have relived another life. It was better, and I was the commencement speaker … I took your advice, and I asked the teacher for help. But was it part of the anesthesia afterlife or was I living an alternative reality?

MARYAMMA. Exactly.

VERONICA. But that was an either-or question. What do you mean, "exactly"?

MARYAMMA. Miss Witherspoon, your aura is looking a little lighter, can you feel it?

VERONICA. I think I can a little. Something was wrong with the weather. Is that reality or was that part of a dream?

MARYAMMA. Exactly. More government study. Always a sign of lies and obfuscation.

VERONICA. Next time, can I have the anesthesia afterlife but no alternative realities? Just a nice rest, you know.

MARYAMMA. I have a treat for you. Someone has asked to speak with you.

VERONICA. Oh?

MARYAMMA. Yes. Look who's here.

(Enter a Black Woman in a flowered dress and a going-to-church hat. She seems friendly and also a bit feisty.)

BLACK WOMAN. Hello.

VERONICA. Hello.

BLACK WOMAN. Hello.

VERONICA. *(Uncertain.)* Hello. Mrs. Donaldson?

BLACK WOMAN. I'm Jesus Christ. I wanted to meet you before you reincarnate for your next life.

VERONICA. *(A bit taken aback; smiles, wonders if she's being kidded.)* You look like the teacher I was just dreaming about.

BLACK WOMAN. Ah, so my appearance to you was foretold in a dream?

VERONICA. Not exactly. Someone who looked like you, but without the hat. She was a teacher. And historically Jesus Christ was a man, was he not?

BLACK WOMAN. I take many forms. Today I'm a black woman. Do you like my hat?

VERONICA. It's okay.

BLACK WOMAN. Really? I think it's nicer than okay, but no matter. I told Maryamma I wanted to speak to you because in your next life I want you to point out to people all the ways that they are not following me.

VERONICA. Well, I was telling Maryamma I'm hoping for more of the anesthesia afterlife.

BLACK WOMAN. I've made a list for you of things I've said that people are ignoring. Number one: Blessed are the meek, for they shall inherit the earth. Number two: Blessed are the merciful, for they shall receive mercy.

VERONICA. Oh yes, the Beatitudes. They're lovely.

BLACK WOMAN. Thank you. Though I mean for them to be lived, not just admired as lovely.

VERONICA. Well, I'm sure everyone understands that.

BLACK WOMAN. Really? Number three: Let him who is without sin, cast the first stone. Likewise, judge not lest ye be judged.

VERONICA. Ah yes. Well, it's hard not to judge, isn't it, it sort of happens automatically, I think.

BLACK WOMAN. The path I ask of people *is* hard. Number four: Love God, and love thy neighbor as thyself.

VERONICA. You know, I'm not really a Christian anymore. I don't know what I am.

BLACK WOMAN. Number five: It is easier for a camel to pass through the eye of a needle than for a rich man to get into heaven.

VERONICA. I see. Is there an income cut-off where that comes into effect?

BLACK WOMAN. No, there's no cut-off. Look at the lilies of the field, and then just have a little bit more than they do, and that'll be fine.

VICTORIA. I see.

BLACK WOMAN. Number six: If thy eye offend thee, pluck it out.

VERONICA. Pluck it out?

BLACK WOMAN. No, that's a hard one. Forget that one. Number seven: What does it profit a man if he gains the whole world, and loses his soul?

VERONICA. Yes, that's a good one.

BLACK WOMAN. *(With friendly encouragement.)* I really need you to get down there and shake these people up!

VERONICA. *(Laughs weakly.)* Oh well, I'm not really much of a messenger. Why don't you go back there and say these things?

BLACK WOMAN. I did that once, now it's somebody else's turn! I look down at people on earth not following what I said, and I just get riled up. *(Starting to get worked up.)* I mean, I said, "blessed are the merciful," right, that's clear, right? I didn't say, blessed are those who proclaim themselves holier than others and read the Book of Revelations as if it's an *instruction* booklet, and sit around waiting for the Rapture, when they think I'm going to bring all these holy folk up to heaven, and we're gonna sit up there together and watch Jews and atheists and non-Christians writhe about in agony for years and years. And we'll watch that as what? — Entertainment? Enjoyable revenge?

VERONICA. The Book of Revelations is a particularly dense book, isn't it? I could never make sense of it.

BLACK WOMAN. That's a pleasingly humble reaction. You see, I'm concerned with the misuse of my name. Answer me a question. Didn't I say blessed are the peacemakers? That's number eight. Blessed are the peacemakers.

VERONICA. Please stop reciting these numbers to me, I'm actually mostly in agreement.

BLACK WOMAN. If you're in agreement, why won't you help?

VERONICA. Well … I don't know, I just don't want to. Besides, people have gotten very comfortable with their own interpretations of Christianity. It would be very hard to budge them, especially if I had to say, oh, and by the way, I was told this by some black woman in a hat who said she was Jesus Christ.

BLACK WOMAN. I'll be a black woman on Tuesday if I want, and a Pakistani man on Wednesday, and a ham sandwich on

Thursday. I'm communicating in parable, plus I also have a sense of humor. *(Harshly.)* Do you like my hat?

VERONICA. It's not my place to fix the world. If you want to fix it, you go down there again and fix it yourself. And you *should* go as a floating ham sandwich; I bet people will really pay attention to you then. But leave me out of it. I have not liked the world, and it has not liked me, and I thought once you died, it was over, and that's what I am, I'm over. Over and out. Got it?

BLACK WOMAN. Got it. *(To Maryamma.)* I thought you said she would be receptive.

MARYAMMA. Oh, give her time.

VERONICA. Give me a lot of time. Eternity, preferably.

MARYAMMA. Oh, look who's coming now.

(Enter Gandalf. Dressed like Ian McKellan in The Lord of the Rings *movies. Gray beard, long white robe, staff. Charismatic, full of wisdom. He has a British accent and a rich, sonorous sound to his speaking voice.)*

Miss Witherspoon, this is Gandalf. He asked to speak with you as well.

GANDALF. Hello, Miss Witherspoon.

VERONICA. Hello. *(Polite.)* And have you met Jesus?

GANDALF. *(To Black Woman.)* Oh yes, of course. Sorry I didn't recognize you. I thought you were Josephine Baker.

BLACK WOMAN. Thank you. I thought you were Rex Harrison.

VERONICA. What?

GANDALF. Well, I do have a British accent.

BLACK WOMAN. I should warn you, she's difficult.

GANDALF. *(Wishing to be the charming diplomat.)* Well, I'm sure she's not difficult, perhaps just … perplexed.

BLACK WOMAN. Oh, she's perplexed alright. *(Gandalf addresses Veronica.)*

GANDALF. Miss Witherspoon, Jesus Christ and I, and Mr. Gandhi, who's not able to be here today, have all been meeting with the souls in the bardo, urging them to move through their spiritual evolution *faster* than they've been doing, because Middle Earth is in danger of extinction, and looking at it from the netherworld, it all seems so unnecessary and pointless and savage. And so we need the souls who are in process to be engaged, they cannot go live through eighty and ninety years and only learn *tiny, tiny* lessons. We need things to move *faster.*

VERONICA. *(To Black Woman/Jesus.)* What did you say about Rex Harrison?

GANDALF. Miss Witherspoon, your disagreements with Mr. Harrison are taking up far too much of your mental energy. Let it go. Let it go.

VERONICA. Yes, but ...

GANDALF. No, let it go. Try it, it's easier than you think. Stop your argument with Mr. Harrison. Just stop. Let it go.

VERONICA. *(Thinks.)* Okay. *(Really thinks about letting it go; thinks some more; lets go.)* Okay. *(Bit surprised, she feels lighter.)*

GANDALF. Now you see we started out life brutally, with no language, no skills, the caveman days, and we focused only on survival. And that went on for several centuries. Then we saw the need for other people, and that strength can come from bonding together, and so then we became tribal. Our group becomes our tribe. Our tribe is the important one, and if there are other tribes, who might want the things we want for our survival, those other tribes become our enemy. And so warfare begins, and tribes become nations, and there are more and more terrible weapons, and scientists invent more and more horrible ways in which to kill people, and the spiritual evolution is taking *too long.* There must be a quantum *leap.* People must move forward *faster.*

BLACK WOMAN. Number nine.

VERONICA. Stop. I'm not a leader. Why are you pushing me about this?

GANDALF. You have more strength than you know, Miss Witherspoon.

BLACK WOMAN. You do. You're using your strength to resist. Use it for something else. Be brave. Not like when you knew your sister wasn't a witch and you didn't speak up for her in the Salem witch trials.

VERONICA. I didn't want to be killed too, is that so terrible?

BLACK WOMAN. You're saying that to someone who was crucified?

MARYAMMA. I thought you didn't remember your life in Salem.

VERONICA. Well, I didn't. But now I do. Are you happy?

MARYAMMA. I'm always happy. *(Pause.)* Let's everybody find a place of calm, everybody's aura is getting a little cloudy. *(Maryamma uses her hands to brush away the air around her head and upper body; what she does look elegant and easy. Gandalf and Black Woman do somewhat similar things, but Gandalf's motions are a bit more min-*

48

imalist, and Black Woman has a larger, somewhat forceful way with aura cleansing. But bottom line, they wave their hands around their head and upper body, in order to "cleanse their auras." Veronica watches this, and then gives it a shot, and does the same thing, but with a certain "I don't believe in this" look on her face. They all finish their cleansing of auras.) Would anyone like some tea?

GANDALF. Yes, I would.

BLACK WOMAN. Do you have Red Zinger? *(Suddenly there is the sound of terrible turbulence. All four people start to shake uncontrollably, as if the whole bardo was shaking like a plane during turbulence. They find it hard to stand in one place.)*

MARYAMMA. Oh, hold on.

VERONICA. What's going on?

GANDALF. Just some turbulence. Hold on.

VERONICA. Turbulence? In the bardo?

GANDALF. Yes. I was hoping this wouldn't happen.

VERONICA. What wouldn't happen?

BLACK WOMAN. We were afraid of this. India and Pakistan have exchanged nuclear attacks, and North Korea has bombed South Korea. And terrorists have set off biological attacks in London, Madrid, Rome, and New York. And the United States has bombed Iraq, Syria, and Iran. And so we're feeling turbulence up here. But don't worry. It will pass, and then we can get back to discussing her next incarnation. *(The turbulence and shaking continues for a bit. Then it stops.)* Oh, thank goodness. It's over, for now at least.

MARYAMMA. Perhaps that tea now.

VERONICA. Wait. "Discuss my next incarnation." I don't want to go back there, especially after what you told me just happened. What does the world look like?

GANDALF. Well, not good. It's funny, all that worry about Russia and the United States and their nuclear stand-off, and then this is how the nuclear nightmare unfolds with all these smaller states, and even individuals, opening Pandora's Box below.

VERONICA. I was always afraid of that myth, Pandora's Box.

GANDALF. With good cause. So in your next reincarnation, Miss Witherspoon, you must work for global understanding … the various tribes must move past their tribal mentalities, and find a way to embrace their interdependence.

BLACK WOMAN. That's right! Move past it!

VERONICA. Well, easier said than done, no?

GANDALF. Your next life, I think you'll be in the Middle East. You will all be dying of radiation poisoning, and you must convince people of the need for non-violence.

VERONICA. I am not Mahatma Gandhi. I am an emotionally damaged woman with poor follow-through and little bravery. And I am not about to be sent back to live in a new Stone Age. I simply refuse.

MARYAMMA. Miss Witherspoon, it is not your soul's right to refuse.

VERONICA. *(Realizes she must come up with an alternative plan.)* Look, I see I wasted those other lives I had. Let me go back there, before these things have happened, and relive one of those lives. And I'll try to do some of what you say.

BLACK WOMAN. "Try" is a bad word. Don't "try" to do it. Do it.

MARYAMMA. Yes, but you can't go back and live a life you've already lived. That's not how it works.

VERONICA. Well, didn't I just relive Ginny's life? Or part of it? And her life got better. Maybe it was a dream, but maybe it wasn't. And what about quantum physics and the speed of light … and … and … "There are more things in heaven and earth, Horatio, than are dreamt of in your … puny little brain." Who says time has to go forward? — Maybe it can go backwards. And didn't one of you say faith can move mountains?

BLACK WOMAN. I think that was Norman Vincent Peale.

VERONICA. Well, he's not the only one who's said it. Others have, too. So I say anything is possible, too. I've stopped my reincarnation several times, which this woman says I shouldn't have been able to do, I say I can reincarnate BACK in time when there's still hope. I don't want to live in what you say you're sending me to.

MARYAMMA. *(Regretfully.)* The bardo has certain rules …

GANDALF. No. Miss Witherspoon is right. If her soul can reincarnate backwards in time, and relive a life better and make the outcome of the world better … we should let her.

MARYAMMA. Well, "let her," sure. But is it actually do-able?

BLACK WOMAN. Maybe I should redo the crucifixion. No, that's too complicated. Never mind.

VERONICA. Yes, I'll go back. I just can't go forward, let me try to clear up the mess in the past … *(Senses Black Woman's disapproval.)* … sorry, I won't use the word "try," let me CLEAR up the mess in the past, and I don't know, I guess from the sound of it, I'm meant to be a pacifist Christian who teaches the importance of breaking down tribal differences.

BLACK WOMAN. And I'm just *one* of the faces of God, include that.

VERONICA. Okay.

GANDALF. Miss Witherspoon, stand in the place from which you shall return to a previous time. *(Veronica goes back to her chair, which is the "usual" spot where the returns to earth have taken place. She stands by the chair, doesn't sit. Black Woman, Gandalf and Maryamma all start to exit, but with their eyes on Veronica as they leave.)*

BLACK WOMAN. Good luck!

GANDALF. You will not be alone. Other souls will follow you back as well.

BLACK WOMAN. In Hartford, Hereford and Hampshire, hurricanes hardly happen. Ask for help.

MARYAMMA. Goodbye, Miss Witherspoon, I'll have that ginger tea ready when you return.

(Veronica is alone on stage now. The "returning to earth" whoosh sounds begin. Veronica's face doesn't struggle, she's resigned and almost willing to go back now. The sounds of "returning to earth" — wind, music, etc. — continue in intensity. As Veronica is about to "whoosh" down to earth, the lights dim to black, and the sounds intensify.)

Scene 19

Lights come back up. We are back in the nursery room of the first baby scene, with the first mother. The mother is found in light, dressed as she was in the first scene, and looking down at the bassinet. Veronica is in the bassinet, in the same bonnet. She's looking out initially, not quite sure where she's going to find herself.

MOTHER. Hello, darling. Hello there. Yes. It's Mommy. Hello. Good morning. How did precious sleep?

VERONICA. *(Her adult self speaking.)* Oh God, did it work? I hope I'm not in Iraq or Syria or something. Where am I? *(Looks around.)*

MOTHER. Hello, darling. Welcome to your home in Connecticut.

VERONICA. Connecticut, thank God! I think this is back in time. I'm pretty sure. *(Speaks as baby.)* Ga ga. Goo goo. Ma-ma-ma! Ma-ma-ma!

MOTHER. One less syllable, dear. Ma-ma. Ma-ma.

VERONICA. Ma-ma-ma. Ma-ma-ma. *(Adult self.)* Oh, God I've got to relearn language. Oh Lord, it takes too long. I better be a prodigy, that's all I can say.

MOTHER. What, dear?

VERONICA. Google, google.

MOTHER. Yes, Google, that's a search engine. Oh, David, she's very chatty this morning. She almost said Mama.

(Enter David, the father. He is in a suit, dressed for work. He, though, also has Gandalf's hair and long beard. And is played by same actor who played Gandalf. His manner of speaking, though, is how he spoke as the original father.)

FATHER. Talkative, is she? Good morning, sweet pea.

MOTHER. Good God, David! When did you grow that beard? And the hair? *(Veronica notices his hair and beard too. And recognizes him as Gandalf.)*

FATHER. Oh, over the last few weeks.

MOTHER. Well, how could I have not noticed it?

FATHER. You've been focused on Miss Witherspoon.

MOTHER. Who?

FATHER. You know, the old nursery rhyme. Whither the spoon goes, whither the fork. Wither-spoon.

MOTHER. I hope you're going to shave. You look like something out of *The Lord of the Rings.*

FATHER. We'll see. What a beautiful baby. *(Sound of dog barking, then growling. Seemingly the dog comes into the room.)*

MOTHER. Oh, David, don't let Fido in here. I think he's jealous of the baby.

FATHER. He's just not used to her yet. He'll learn to accept her.

MOTHER. Well, he doesn't usually show his teeth.

FATHER. He'll get used to her, if we just let them spend time together.

VERONICA. *(Firmly, commanding, she who must be obeyed.)* GET THE DAMN DOG OUTTA HERE! *(Mother and Father look very startled.)*

MOTHER. David? Did she say words?

FATHER. I don't think so. She sounded very firm though.

MOTHER. I feel like she told us to get the dog out of here.

FATHER. Well, maybe she's right. Let's keep the dog out of this room. Come on, Fido. *(Father takes dog out.)*

VERONICA. *(Adult self, to herself.)* Okay, I need to learn language now. *(Baby; speaks clearly though.)* A, E, I, O, U. Aaaaaaa. Eeeeeeeee. I-iiiiiii. O-oooooooo. *(Father comes backs in.)*

MOTHER. David, she just said the vowels.

FATHER. Babies make lots of vowel sounds.

MOTHER. No, in an organized way. She said A, E, I, O, U.

VERONICA. A, E, I, O, U.

FATHER. By George, she's got it! By George, she's got it!

VERONICA. *(Adult self.)* Oh God, it's Rex Harrison again. *(Whispers to Father/Gandalf.)* You better be nicer this time.

FATHER. Very well, I will.

MOTHER. What?

FATHER. Nothing. Well, this is clearly a prodigy baby. I can tell it's going to learn language very soon. Whither the spoon, whither the fork, the baby's a gift, brought here by the stork.

MOTHER. I've never heard that rhyme.

VERONICA. Ga ga. Ma-ma-ma. Google, google. Gee gee gee gee gee. *(Pointedly.)* Global. Global. Glo-bal.

MOTHER. She keeps making words. I'm a little confused.

FATHER. Well, she's going to be smart, that's all.

MOTHER. Oh, a smart baby. I might just prefer a happy baby.

FATHER. Well, there may be more need for a smart baby. Come on, let's hear the vowels again. A, E, I, O, U.

VERONICA. *(Very fast.)* A, E, I, O, U. In Hartford, Hereford and Hampshire.

FATHER. Hurricanes hardly happen.

VERONICA. Ga ga ga. Google. Alternative forms of energy. Consensus. Mediation. Diplomacy. Ga ga. Blblblblblbblblblll. *(Maryamma enters, carrying a tray with tea on it.)*

MARYAMMA. I thought you might like some tea. *(Veronica does recognize Maryamma, just as she recognized the "Gandalf-ness" of the father moments ago.)*

MOTHER. Oh thank you, Raini. David, I don't think you've met Raini. I hired her yesterday.

FATHER. Yes, while I was growing my beard. How do you do?

MARYAMMA. Do you like ginger tea?

FATHER. Yes, thank you.

MARYAMMA. *(Looks at Veronica.)* What a pretty baby.

FATHER. She's very smart.

MOTHER. Well, all parents think their baby is smart.

VERONICA. In order to survive, we must find a way to break through the centuries of stressing tribal differences, and evolve to finding tribal and human similarities. *(All are startled.)*

MARYAMMA. She speaks in complete sentences already.

MOTHER. I know. It's unusual.

FATHER. Well, she's anxious to make a mark in the world.

MARYAMMA. What a lovely clear aura she has. *(Maryamma, Father and Mother stare down at the baby.)*

(Veronica looks up at them. Then she looks outward. The lights dim, but a special light stays on Veronica's face longer than on the others. Her face is the last thing we see before the lights dim to black. Her expression is a little hard to read, but it contains hope and worry. Or maybe worry and hope.)

End of Play